INSPIRING GUIDES

Joy

100 Affirmations for Happiness

Elicia Rose

ROCK
POINT

For Alex, who sparks joy within
me like no one else.

Contents

Introduction

The quest for happiness is as old as time. If you ask most people what they want to experience more of in life, you can bet that happiness will be one of the most popular answers. We strive to experience as much joy and fulfillment as possible, yet what exactly is happiness? And how do we begin to cultivate more of it in our daily lives?

Happiness, broadly defined as a state of well-being and contentment, is a highly subjective experience and feels unique to each person. Although I don't believe there is a universal definition for happiness, I do believe we all have the capacity to increase our own feelings of joy, whatever that might look like to us on an individual level.

Rather than tackling the philosophical debate surrounding the meaning of happiness, my take is a little simpler. I can't tell you what happiness looks like across all humans, but I believe we each have the power to develop our mind-set to cultivate more happiness in our lives.

Let me begin by telling you what I believe happiness *isn't*. I don't think we can find true happiness in things. Of course, we all enjoy material items, and although they may bring feelings of excitement and joy, it doesn't take long before these feelings fade, and we focus on the next thing we want to attain. This isn't all our fault. Society is geared in a way that encourages us to always want more and never feel quite satisfied with what we have. I don't think we need to give everything away, and I definitely think we can all enjoy material comforts, but I do believe seeing them for what they are helps our well-being in the long term.

I also think that happiness isn't some grand and elusive concept that can only be attained after sitting in meditation for hours or completing some personal quest. I believe that happiness is found in the small things: the quiet, daily moments that make our hearts feel full. This will look different for every person. It might be found in watching the sunset, seeing your pet after a long day at work, or that first sip of your morning cup of tea. These small moments provide us with the opportunity to be grateful for how blessed we truly are. When we begin to focus on the little things, we realize that happiness isn't so unattainable after all.

I believe tools such as positive affirmations, journaling, and meditation are all helpful in creating huge positive changes in your life. Just one simple affirmation has the power to completely change your day. I first realized how important affirmations were when I started using them while I was at university. I began to share affirmations and illustrations on social media through my business, Bloom Affirmations, with the hope of inspiring and motivating others. Now I am proud to say that I have encouraged numerous people all over the world to shift their mind-set and focus on creating more joy in their lives.

The following affirmations and exercises are written to help you begin to cultivate feelings of joy and contentment on a daily basis. When we use tools such as affirmations, we increase our self-awareness and begin to get in touch with what really matters to us. Take your time with each exercise and find a way to make affirmations work for you. This might include speaking them aloud, writing them in your journal, or setting reminders on your phone to repeat them to yourself.

I believe that every single one of us has the ability to feel content, no matter what we have experienced. You don't need to earn the right to be happy; it's something that is your birth right, and taking the time to find what brings you joy doesn't make you selfish. Believing you are worthy of finding happiness is a big step in shaping your life in a way that is more fulfilling. We all deserve to live a life that is gratifying and in alignment with what truly matters to us.

Gratitude is also a key factor when it comes to joy. We are on this planet for such a short amount of time, and sometimes being thankful is all you need to make you realize that you already have a lot in your life to be happy about (more on that later). We all experience struggles and difficult times and pushing through them with a false sense of positivity is never a good decision. Stopping and noticing when things are pretty good, however, can help promote a more joyful outlook on life. Being grateful for the little things, as well as the big things in life, always helps me feel more content.

My hope is that this book connects you to your true self and shows you what is important in life. We all deserve to feel joy and contentment, no matter what we've gone through. I hope you are able to ignite that spark within you and begin living your life in alignment with what truly matters.

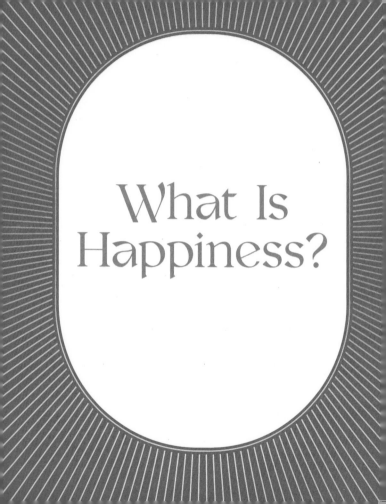

What Is Happiness?

The first step in increasing feelings of joy and happiness involves turning our attention inward and realizing what matters in life. Happiness is an inside job, and if you spend time looking for it in people, places, or things, it won't be sustainable.

The way we live our life and who we share it with are of course essential to our happiness and well-being, but I believe it is the way we internalize these situations that creates true happiness. Life is constantly changing, and we can't predict the future. People and opportunities may come and go, and if a huge part of our happiness is dependent on external circumstances, it's likely we will experience even more pain when things change.

When we choose to make happiness an inside job, we naturally increase feelings of calmness and stability. We become aware of what really matters and make peace with the unpredictable nature of life. When we decide to stop outsourcing our happiness, it takes the pressure off our loved ones. It's never anyone else's job to make us happy. The responsibility to develop awareness and inner peace always lies within us.

The following affirmations and exercises are designed to help you understand what happiness means to you, and how to turn your attention inward to make happiness an inside job.

Happiness is a choice I decide to make every day

The idea of happiness being a choice might seem strange, but when we think of happiness in this way, it gives us a lot more personal freedom. Rather than allowing external forces to shape us, we can decide to be the master of how we think and feel.

What choice can you make today that will help you feel 1 percent happier?

My happiness is my responsibility

We often place a lot of pressure on things, people, and events to decide how we feel without even realizing it. Deciding to be responsible for your own levels of happiness makes you much more resilient to whatever might be happening around you. Of course, we will be influenced by external factors because we don't live in isolation, but we can choose to interpret external influences in a way that helps us rather than being at the mercy of them.

In what ways have you been outsourcing your happiness? Who and what have you been placing pressure on to make you happy? Make a list.

I release the pressure I place on others to fulfil my happiness

In relationships of all kinds we all have needs that we deserve to have met, but if we don't express our feelings, tension begins to build. Uncommunicated needs quickly lead to resentment. It's time to be honest with yourself and shine a light on what you might have been ignoring.

Look again at the list you wrote for the journal prompt on page 18. For each person you listed, explore further in your journal how you have placed pressure on them to make you happy. If you haven't, consider making some notes about what you would like to communicate to this person.

As I turn my attention inward, I learn about what matters to me

Many of us fall into the trap of thinking that how our lives look from the outside will define our levels of happiness. Social media certainly doesn't help, as we compare ourselves to everyone else's highlights. It's time to think about what really matters to you on a deeper level.

What truly matters to you in life? Make a list of everything that is important to you. You might include people, places, and things, but also include values, such as freedom, growth, peace, and so on.

I find joy in the little things

Happiness doesn't need to be a grand concept. Huge life events certainly have the power to make us feel very happy, but joy can be found in the small, daily actions that pass by unnoticed.

Think about the small things that you do on a daily basis that put a smile on your face. What little things light you up?

As I connect to the anchor within, I allow the ups and downs of life to pass with ease

The visual of having an inner anchor can help you feel grounded no matter what's happening in your life. Imagine that you are so anchored to the core of your being that whatever happens, you'll always be okay.

Complete this sentence: Now that I am choosing to make happiness an inside job and connect to the anchor within, I will . . .

I am reminded of the things that make me happy on a daily basis

Placing visual cues in your environment to spark happiness is a great way to keep returning to joy, no matter how your day goes.

Gather your favorite photos, quotes, and images to make a happiness vision board. Include everything that fills you with joy, including loved ones, pets, places, experiences, and anything else that instantly makes you feel good. Place this vision board somewhere that you'll see it every day. You can also create a digital collage if you prefer and set it as the wallpaper on your phone.

I might not control what happens, but I do control how I react

Trying to control all the external circumstances around you is not only a waste of time, but it's also the quickest way to feel unhappy and powerless. The only thing we ever really have control over is how we react to the world around us.

Think about one situation you are currently facing that is causing you to feel unsettled. What thoughts and emotions do you currently have around this situation? Is there a way you could view the situation differently to maintain your inner peace?

Today I choose to make happiness an inside job

Making happiness an inside job means that instead of looking to things outside yourself to make you happy, you choose to make happiness your responsibility.

What do you look toward to make you happy or distract you from how you're really feeling? Popular examples include food, alcohol, shopping, and dating, to name a few. How could you develop a more balanced relationship with these things?

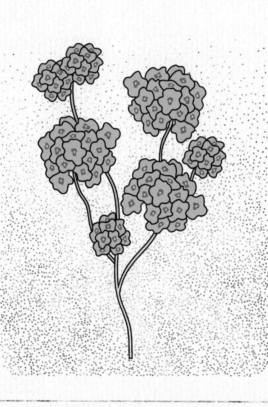

I foster a deep sense of inner peace

Happiness comes from having a sense of inner peace, which can be cultivated in the same way that a new skill can be developed. It might take some time to find out what makes you truly happy, but keep trying new things until you find something.

Do one thing today for yourself and completely by yourself that will make you feel good. Some of my favorite choices? A walk in nature, a bubble bath, or ordering pizza and watching my favorite film!

I learn about what truly matters to me and release what doesn't

When you find out what truly matters to you, it's easier to stop getting caught up in the things that aren't really important.

What have you been getting caught up in recently that doesn't really matter as much as you think? Make a list of the little things you have been stressing about that have taken up too much of your time or energy. Once you have written this list, cross out each sentence and write, "I forgive myself for getting swept up in this."

I deserve to be happy

No matter what you've gone through, you absolutely deserve to be happy. Your happiness is important, and you matter.

Complete this sentence: I deserve to feel happy, grounded, calm, and at peace because . . .

I am ready to let more happiness come into my life

Being open to the possibility of more happiness allows life to surprise you with unexpected gifts. Taking small, daily actions to support your happiness can have wonderful effects.

List three actions you can take on a daily basis that would help invite more happiness into your life.

The more I connect with myself, the more I learn about what makes me happy

When you were a child, you played and laughed and enjoyed yourself without much thought. There were certain activities that filled you with pure happiness.

What did you love to do as a child? What brought you more joy than anything else? If you're struggling to answer this, ask your family or imagine what happiness would have been like for you as a child.

I invite my inner child to express and play

Life doesn't have to be so serious all the time. Expressing your inner child is a great way to move away from a stressed or busy mind.

Connect to your inner child by taking some time today to dance, sing, play, or be silly.

I nurture the seeds of happiness within my soul. I allow them to bloom brightly

There are gifts and talents inside of you just waiting to be expressed. You could really make a difference to this world if you began nurturing yourself.

What is inside you, waiting to be expressed or created? Maybe you've always wanted to start a blog or showcase your photography. Think about something you would really love to express or create and write down three actionable steps you could take to begin the process.

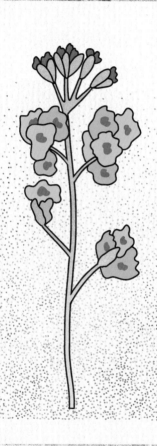

I choose to be happy in this present moment. I make peace with my past

There are things in the past that you might wish had not happened. We've all experienced hurt and pain. What we choose to do with it, however, is up to us.

What situations from the past still continue to have an impact on your life? Be honest with yourself as you journal about these experiences. Once you have done this, reflect on each event and ask yourself: Is it possible to make peace with this situation so it no longer affects my present moment?

Starting from today, I welcome more joy, laughter, and happiness into my life

One of the quickest ways to feel happier is to have a good laugh about something. Laughter is the ultimate medicine and the expression of pure joy.

Make a list of all the things that make you belly laugh. It might be certain films or videos, people, or memories. Allow yourself to smile as you remember these things.

I am in charge of my day

Creating your mind-set in the morning is a great way to invite more joy and happiness into your day. Use this affirmation for a boost of self-confidence in the morning.

Write this affirmation on a sticky note and leave it next to your coffee machine, in the bathroom, or any other place that you'll see it soon after you've woken up. Let it act as a reminder that you're in charge of how today turns out. Even if things don't turn out as you'd hoped, you are still in charge of how you react.

I radiate happiness

Joy is infectious. As you work to become happier, you will naturally start making those around you feel good.

In what ways do you make a positive impact on the world around you? Think about the ways you help your family and friends, make a difference at work, or any other activities that help make this world a kinder place.

I make happiness a top priority

It is not selfish to make happiness a top priority. Happiness and joy have the power to change this world. By giving yourself permission to prioritize your own happiness, you inspire others to do the same.

Where do cultivating feelings of joy and happiness currently rank in your list of priorities? Is there any way you can rearrange your priorities to focus on things that make you happier?

I ride the waves of life with an open heart

Life is going to take you on a journey whether you like it or not. Make the decision to flow through life with an open and accepting nature rather than resisting it.

How can you move through your day with a more open and loving heart?

My heart guides me to joy and happiness

Your heart possesses wisdom that sometimes can't be explained or rationalized. Follow it anyway, and allow it to lead you to more joy.

Try this connecting with your heart exercise. Close your eyes and place your hands over your heart. Take a few slow, deep breaths, focusing on this area. What messages does your heart have for you?

I am ready to make happiness a permanent quality in my life

Happiness doesn't have to be a fleeting feeling that you are lucky to experience. It can become a much more permanent fixture in your life, if only you invite it in.

Do you believe you deserve to experience happiness on a daily basis? If not, why?

I am happy, grounded, calm, and at peace

Make the decision that, just for today, you'll focus on inviting more of these feelings into your daily activities.

Create a happiness mind map. Write down the words happy, grounded, calm, and at peace on a large piece of paper. Expand on each word to include the people, places, practices, and things that make you feel this way. Write down anything that comes to mind and don't worry if it looks messy. You can also turn this into a creative activity by adding color or doodles. Keep this piece of paper in the front of your journal so you can refer to it whenever you need a reminder. You might also wish to create a digital version, if you prefer.

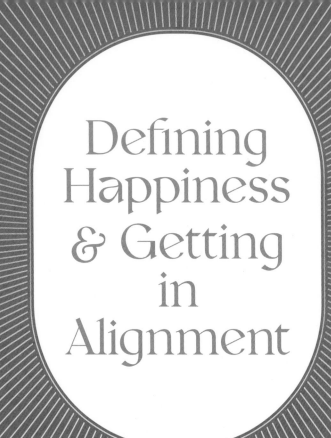

Defining
Happiness
& Getting
in
Alignment

Now that we have spent some time practicing making happiness an inside job, it's time to understand what happiness means to us on an individual level. What brings one person so much joy (going on a run, for example) might cause another person to feel the exact opposite. If you're lucky enough to have the basics covered, such as a roof over your head, food in your belly, and people around you who care, you will also have the opportunity to spend time thinking about what makes you truly happy.

If we don't know what brings us joy and happiness, then it's difficult to know what changes we need to make in order to increase these feelings. This section is all about creating your own definition of happiness, then examining how your current lifestyle fits in with this. Developing a level of self-awareness about what truly matters to us and knowing how much we are in alignment with this is a great way to increase overall feelings of contentment.

Be honest with yourself as you work with the following affirmations and journal prompts. We are often so busy that we rarely stop to think about these things, so I encourage you to take your time with each exercise. If you feel any resistance come up, know that you absolutely deserve to shape your life to increase feelings of happiness. These changes don't have to be drastic, and you might find that just a few small changes will have a noticeable impact. As always, allow your intuition to guide you. You know yourself better than anyone else.

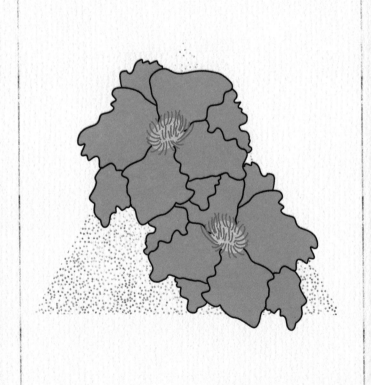

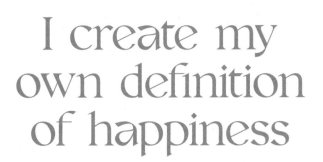

I create my own definition of happiness

What does happiness look like to you? What does happiness feel like to you? How do you express happiness?

Create a spider diagram of all the characteristics, values, actions, and feelings that happiness brings up for you.

I release societal expectations and follow what makes me truly happy

Whether we realize it or not, we all face societal pressure. We all integrate ideas about how we should live our lives. This might include how we should look and dress, the job we should have, whether or when we should get married and have children, among many other things. We can choose to create our own time line rather than allowing society to dictate how we should live our lives.

What societal pressures have you been under and is this really the way you want to live your life?

I allow myself to feel desire

Wanting things for yourself is not bad! Having desire is normal, and acknowledging your needs is healthy. Empowering yourself to desire the things you want permits more happiness to enter your life.

What do you desire for yourself but have pushed down or ignored? This might include a better job, a different relationship, or a change in where you live.

It is safe for me to reflect on what makes me happy

Reflecting on what makes you happy might bring up feelings of self-indulgence or judgment. Rather than allowing these feelings to take over, explore what might be causing them.

Make a list of all the limiting thoughts you have around why you don't deserve to be happy and why you shouldn't reflect on your own happiness. Once you have done this, cross out each one and write, "It is safe for me to release this thought and focus on what makes me happy."

I deserve to feel content every day

If happiness seems too far out of reach for you, try working with the feeling of being content. To me, contentment is strongly linked to a feeling of inner peace.

Make a list of all the things that make you feel content, joyful, or at peace. Look at your list and see whether there are any options that you could incorporate on a daily basis. One of my favorite options? Making matcha latte using my milk frother. It's the simple things!

I am honest with myself about the things that don't make me happy

When was the last time you were honest with yourself about the causes of your unhappiness? We tend to suppress these thoughts rather than examine them.

What current habits, routines, people, or practices are in your life at the moment that you know don't make you feel good? Of the ones that are in your control, what steps can you take to minimize their effect?

I give the pursuit of my happiness the respect and attention it deserves

Respecting the pursuit of happiness is a reflection of the respect you have for yourself. Are you willing to give it the attention it deserves?

List three to five actions you can implement to start taking your happiness and joy seriously.

The more I show up for my own happiness, the more happiness will show up for me

Sometimes we think that joy and happiness should come to us, without effort on our part. The truth is, if we want anything in life, we need to do the inner work, take action, and show up for ourselves.

How have you been expecting happiness to come to you? What actions can you take to help meet happiness halfway so that it shows up more in your life?

I pursue things that truly matter to me

Your dreams are important, and you deserve to pursue them. It's also important that you work toward dreams that matter to you, and not to anyone else.

What is a big goal or dream of yours? Why is this important to you? What steps can you take/are already taking to bring yourself closer to this vision?

I examine my actions closely and work to change any that are not conducive to my own happiness

Self-sabotage is real, and we are all capable of getting in our own way to stop ourselves from living a fulfilled life. Think about some of your habits or behaviors that might be blocking your own happiness. Once you have made a list, write down the reasons why you might engage in them.

It is safe for me to release fear

We all experience fear and its many faces. From low-level uneasiness to full-on dread, fear keeps us stuck, scared, and playing small.

When you think about creating a happier life for yourself, do you experience any fear? If so, journal these thoughts and feelings and examine where they might be coming from.

I am worthy of love, happiness, and joy

If there were only one affirmation I could recommend out of the whole book, it would be this one. No matter who you are, you absolutely deserve to experience the good things in life.

Write this affirmation on your mirror, place it on your fridge door, or set it as your phone wallpaper. Refer to this affirmation throughout your day, speaking it aloud if possible. Every time you say it, place your hands on your heart and connect to the loving energy that already exists within you.

I shape my life to include more joy

There will always be mundane or boring aspects of your day, as life can't be amazing 100 percent of the time. You, however, have the opportunity to inject some fun into these activities.

Think of some weekly activities that are dull or tedious, yet unavoidable. Think about how you could make them more fun or engaging. Some examples include playing your favorite music as you clean the house or taking yourself out for a coffee as you work through life admin.

As I focus on small changes, the bigger things take care of themselves

Never underestimate the power of small changes to radically improve many other areas of your life. Beginning your day with a five-minute meditation will help you feel focused and calm, but over time, it could also help improve the quality of your relationships, work-life balance, and your confidence levels.

What is one small change you could implement from today on?

I am ready to get in alignment with the boldest, most ambitious vision of my life

It is okay for you to dream big. It is okay for you to have ambitions. It is okay for you to think outside the box. Not only is it okay, but it should be actively encouraged!

If you could shape your life EXACTLY as you'd like, without any limitations or worries, what would it look like? Think big here. Journal the boldest, most ambitious life you could possibly imagine.

I go about my day with a playful and lighthearted energy

We can all fall into the trap of taking life too seriously. The truth is, every situation doesn't have to be so solemn or deep.

What situations have you been thinking way too deeply about? What are you gaining from overthinking? How can you reframe this situation with a sense of lightheartedness?

I determine my own version of joy

You are truly unique, and what brings you joy will also be unique. Sometimes we disconnect from the things that bring us joy because we worry about what our loved ones might think. Let's begin releasing some of this judgment.

Answer this question honestly in your journal: Is your current version of joy what truly makes you happy, or is it influenced by what your loved ones would approve of?

I am willing to make positive and beneficial changes

Any type of change requires some form of mental or physical effort, which might not always feel easy in the beginning.

Are you willing to experience the initial resistance in order to experience long-term gains?

I make changes from a place of loving-kindness

Changes made from a place of loving-kindness are very different from changes made from a place of unworthiness. If we believe we need fixing and must change something in order to become worthy, then all we do is reinforce the belief that we aren't good enough as we are. This is why it is so important to make changes with a loving and kind attitude toward ourselves.

Examine the changes you are currently making in your life. Are they coming from a place of already being good enough or a need to try to become more worthy?

It is okay for me to change my mind

Give yourself permission to change your mind without having to justify yourself. Opinions change and people grow, and you don't need to explain yourself.

Are there any aspects of your life that you continue with simply because you fear judgment or criticism (from yourself or others) if things were to change? Examples include staying in a job that doesn't fulfill you, keeping up with an exercise routine even though it bores you, or maintaining friendships that make you feel drained.

I am kind to myself, especially on difficult days

Making positive and lasting change is never a straightforward journey. Some days will feel easy, productive, and satisfying, and others will feel difficult and more frustrating. This is okay, and to be expected.

If you're having a day where you find yourself slipping into old habits, choose to be kind to yourself rather than berating or criticizing yourself. Come back to this affirmation on those difficult days to remember to give yourself some love.

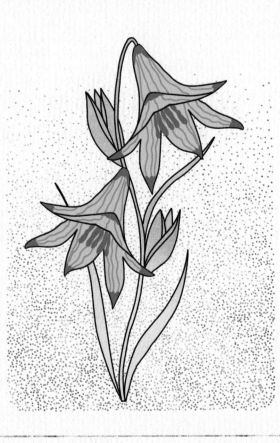

I am capable of more than I give myself credit for

You are more capable and resilient than you know. Even when you doubt yourself, you have reserves of strength and courage that might surprise you.

Make a list of all the times you have made positive changes in your life or overcame something that was challenging. Include small changes as well as big ones.

Every day, I take another step toward leading a more fulfilled life

Twenty-four hours doesn't seem like a lot, but you can make some big leaps in that time.

Try this future life visualization technique. You can complete this exercise in a seated position or lying down. The recommended time is between five and fifteen minutes. Close your eyes and begin to turn your attention inward. Once you feel relaxed, imagine your life one year from now if you keep making positive changes to increase your levels of happiness. Imagine what your relationships, work, leisure time, finances, hobbies, and any other projects could look like if you remain consistent. Enjoy the feelings of joy and excitement that begin to rise.

I value myself and my happiness

You might have noticed a lot of affirmations and exercises centered around worthiness, but there is a good reason for this. Integrating the belief that you are already worthy is one of the most important changes you can ever make.

Complete this sentence: I deserve to feel good about myself and I am worthy of happiness because . . .

I believe happiness is possible for me, no matter what I have experienced

Everything we experience, no matter how painful, contains a powerful lesson from which we can grow and become much wiser. It might take days, months, or years to move through the pain, and that's okay. Know that eventually there is light.

Do you believe happiness is possible for you, despite these things? If you answered no, consider the ways in which you could increase feelings of happiness while working through whatever still needs to be processed.

Developing a Gratitude Mind-set

I f I could pick only one tool that has the power to radically change your mind-set, it would be gratitude. Developing a gratitude mind-set is a quick and effective way to feel happier and more joyful on a daily basis. It seems pretty simple, but how exactly is it so effective?

Gratitude is defined as the quality of being thankful and appreciative. You can be grateful for the big things, like your family, friends, and career, but you can also be grateful for the little things, such as a really good cup of coffee. So often it's our default mind-set to look for what's wrong and resort to criticism. If you look hard enough, you'll notice the flaws in pretty much everything, but if you look hard enough, you'll also notice something to be grateful for, even in bad situations.

Perspective really is everything. What might bring you stress and anxiety (a demanding job, for example) might be exactly what somebody else would love to experience. Frustrated with your partner for forgetting to do the things you asked? At least you have a significant other who loves you, even if they don't get it right all the time.

Developing a gratitude mind-set isn't about painting over all of your problems with a fake attitude of appreciation. It is important that you do address what is concerning you and seek solutions. Gratitude, however, can help you shift your perspective. All of the affirmations in this chapter may not resonate with your current situation, and that is perfectly fine. Repeat the ones that resonate the most with you.

I have woken up to a new day, and for this I am grateful

If you have woken up this morning, you are more fortunate than the thousands worldwide who did not. You have the greatest opportunity of all: another twenty-four hours on this planet. Nothing is promised to us, so make the most of it.

How can you make the most of the next twenty-four hours?

I am thankful for the roof over my head

Your house or space might not be perfect, but you are more fortunate than a good percentage of the global population who don't have this luxury.

Think about your home environment. What do you like the most about it?

I am grateful for the love and support in my life

We don't go through life alone, and it's our support network that keeps us going through tough times. This might include your family, friends, colleagues, partners, or any other loved ones.

How does love and support show up in your life?

I am healthy
I am strong
I am energetic

You don't realize just how important your health is until you lose it. Illness has the potential to knock you off your feet and change your life beyond recognition. If you are healthy, this is a huge thing to be grateful for.

Write a thank you letter to your body for all the ways it keeps you healthy, happy, and supported.

I stop taking the little luxuries for granted and recognize how blessed I am

There are so many daily actions we take that are such luxuries and we don't even realize it. Taking a shower, cooking food, using the internet, and so many other activities are huge blessings.

What little luxuries do you take for granted? Make a list in your journal.

I am thankful for the animals in my life

Animals bring so much joy. For me, there's nothing better than sitting on the sofa and snuggling my cats and dogs. Whether you have pets or choose to observe animals from afar, there's no doubt that they are huge blessings.

Write a gratitude list of all the animals that have impacted your life. You might include pets, from childhood to current, or even animals on the news or social media that have made you smile.

I am grateful for this beautiful planet we call home

Think of all the sunsets, sunrises, mountains, volcanoes, lakes, forests, deserts, oceans, beaches, fields, trees, flowers, and wildlife you have seen in your life. Mother Nature certainly knows how to create something breathtakingly beautiful.

What element of nature has had the biggest impact on you?

As others show unexpected kindness to me, I show unexpected kindness to others

Random acts of kindness have the potential to make your whole day, week, or month, and I am sure you probably have experienced an unexpected gesture that made you feel warm inside. Equally, performing random acts of kindness yourself makes you feel just as good.

Think about a time someone did something unexpected for you that was very kind. How did it make you feel? What is a random act of kindness you could do for a loved one?

I greatly appreciate the technology that makes my everyday life so much easier

Think of how many pieces of technology you use throughout your day that make it so much easier for you to complete tasks or communicate with others. From the internet that allows you to access information at the click of a button, to the electric kettle that makes your morning tea, we are surrounded by technology and gadgets that give us an amazing quality of life.

What pieces of technology do you use throughout your day that you would be lost without?

I see the good in every situation

Tragedies happen. Upsetting events can come out of left field. Even minor disturbances can have a negative impact on our mood. This is part of life, and it's important to know that a lot of it is random, and definitely unexpected. The question is how we react to it.

What is a difficult situation that you are currently facing that could actually hold a valuable lesson? Or alternatively, is there something that has happened in your past that you learned from?

I am grateful for the lessons that almost broke me, because they were the most powerful lessons of all

You are still here despite everything you've gone through, which shows you also possess a deep resilience.

What is one thing you never thought you'd overcome but you did? What did it teach you about yourself?

I am proud of the unique qualities I possess that make me who I am

You are truly unique. There's no one on the planet quite like you. Your combination of skills, talents, qualities, and traits make you one of a kind, and this is something that you should be grateful for.

Make a list of all the skills and qualities that make you unique. Include the things you might have judged or felt embarrassed about at one point in your life. Know that every aspect of you is worthy of recognition.

I am thankful for the experience of romantic love

There's a reason why so many films, books, and music are centered around romance. There's no feeling quite like falling in love. It might not always be like the films depict (and quite rightly so—romantic love is so much deeper than that), but it's certainly something to cherish.

If you have a special person in your life, write them a note or letter including everything you appreciate about them and why you're grateful they are in your life. If you don't, make a list of all the qualities you would like a potential partner to have, and why they are important to you.

I am thankful for the delight of delicious food

Food is amazing. Think of the flavors you can experience and the joy you get from eating a delicious meal. It also sustains and nourishes us, which is so important. I believe one of the greatest gifts of being human is the amazing sense of taste.

What are your favorite foods, drinks, meals, and snacks?

I love being able to exercise

There's no doubt about it—moving your body feels good. Whether you prefer to hike, lift weights, or take a dance class, there are so many ways you can move your body that have just as many mental benefits as physical ones. And it's a great way to show some appreciation to your body.

What forms of movement/exercise bring you the most joy? Do you currently make enough time for these activities?

I am grateful for the opportunity to help others

No matter how problematic your life might seem, there are always others in much worse positions than you. You often don't have to look far to find someone who is struggling in some way.

Do something kind and helpful for someone in need today without asking for anything in return. This might be for a family member, friend, or a stranger. If you need inspiration, visit the Random Acts of Kindness Foundation.

Everything I have experienced has shaped me into the amazing person I am today

All the struggles, tears, and setbacks have shaped you into the resilient, wise, and confident person you are presently.

Practice this "thanking your problems" meditation. Get comfy in a place where you won't be disturbed and close your eyes. Begin to slow your breathing and relax your body. Enter a calm and peaceful state. Place your hands over your heart and begin to bring the problems you're currently experiencing to mind. For each issue, say this statement aloud: "I am grateful for . . . because . . ." This helps cultivate the skill of seeing every experience as a valuable lesson.

I appreciate the gift of laughter

There's nothing quite like having a good laugh, the kind where you can barely catch your breath, your shoulders shake, and you feel so much joy. Laughter has the power to transform your mood and is also a great way of getting rid of excess energy.

The next time you feel yourself getting stressed, watch a funny video, the sillier the better, and have a good laugh. It's a great way to instantly feel better.

I am thankful for the unexpected gifts that show up in my life

It's great when life throws unexpected gifts your way. It might be something small, like the perfect parking space, or something big, like an unexpected sum of money. Life is always giving gifts, if only we stop to take notice.

What unexpected gifts have entered your life? How did they make you feel? Include the small gifts as well as the big ones.

I give thanks for the inspiration that surrounds me

You don't have to look far to find inspiration. It might be via social media, the people you know, or your environment, but inspiration is to be found everywhere.

What is currently inspiring you, and what actions does it make you want to take?

I cherish the gift of travel

Visiting new places, whether locally or further afield, is such a blessing. The opportunity to experience a new environment, culture, or history expands our mind-set in so many ways.

Create a travel wish list. Include all the places you would love to visit. Get specific and include certain cities, locations, venues, or events.

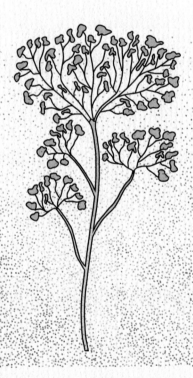

I am thankful for the ability to learn

Education is one of the most powerful tools available for us to transform our lives. Whether this includes formal education or more informal ways such as reading or online courses, accessing knowledge is easier than ever before.

What ways of learning (both formal and informal) have helped shape who you are today? You might also wish to reflect on life experiences that turned out to be a form of education.

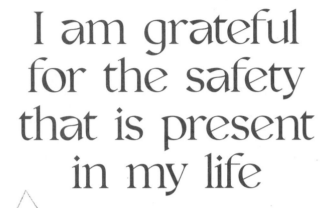

I am grateful for the safety that is present in my life

Most of us are fortunate to live in environments where we are safe. We don't have to worry about conflict or meeting basic needs because they are taken care of. Others certainly aren't this fortunate. Everything might not be perfect, but if you're safe, it really is a big blessing.

Have you been taking the safety and stability of your environment for granted? If so, what can you do to acknowledge how fortunate you are?

I love and appreciate the special people in my life

It's the people in our lives who make everything worthwhile. We all have special people who make our days so much brighter. Your special person might be your partner, best friend, or family member.

Write a thank you note to a special person in your life. Thank them for all that they do and let them know how grateful you are that they are in your life. Give this note to your special person and see how good it makes them feel.

I harness the power of perspective to see what really matters in life

Something that might seem like a big deal at first doesn't seem so overwhelming when you change the way you think about it. Take something like losing your job, for example. At first this could be seen as a highly stressful event that has the potential to damage your self-esteem. However, what if losing your job turns out to be a blessing in disguise by leading you to find a job that is much more fulfilling? Perspective is a valuable tool to help us work out what truly matters in life. What areas of your life could benefit from a little perspective?

Collective
Happiness

Our own happiness is very important, but it's not the full picture. If you were unbelievably happy, yet the people closest to you were suffering, how would that impact you? We don't live in a vacuum, and the well-being of others should matter to us. It's important to think about the happiness of others, whether in our immediate circle or wider collective.

It isn't our job to make others happy, but when we decide to do kind things for others, we can increase their happiness as well as our own. Exploring the topic of happiness wouldn't be complete without considering what we can do to help others and make this world a kinder place. Therefore, in this section, you'll find a range of affirmations and exercises designed to help you become more altruistic and concerned with the well-being of others.

Don't underestimate how much good you can do in this one precious life. You have the power to create really important change, not just for yourself but for others as well. When we make the journey toward happiness a collective journey, we all benefit. Choose things that matter to you and work toward them to make the world a better place.

Collective happiness is important to me

You can create your own definition of collective happiness. For some, it might include just close family members, and for others, it might include a much wider range of people. When you see the people you care about happy, you can't help but feel good yourself.

Whose happiness is important to you? Make a list of all the people you love to see happy.

I can make this world a better place

You have so much potential to instigate change. Whether you choose to focus on your little corner of the world or reach out across borders, you really can make a difference. What causes are you passionate about and why?

I feel good when I choose to help others

There's no doubt about it; when you help others, you also feel good. Altruism (the act of helping others without any expectation of anything in return) warms our hearts and reminds us of the good in human nature.

What is one altruistic act you can do today? Make sure you don't ask for or expect anything in return.

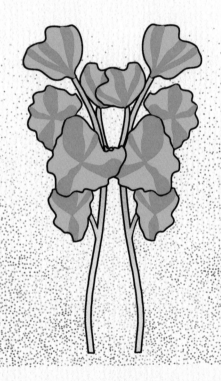

I decide to see the best in people

It can be tempting to view humans through a negative lens. It's so easy to jump to conclusions and judge or criticize others, and see the worst in those around us. In reality, this mind-set isn't effective or conducive to happiness.

Do you tend to see the best or the worst in people? If you tend to see the worst, how does this mind-set affect your own levels of happiness? What could you do to move toward a more optimistic viewpoint? Or alternatively, write down all the good qualities that the people in your life have.

I realize that the smallest acts of kindness can have a big impact

You don't have to drop everything and commit every spare minute to a charitable organization (although if that's your thing, amazing!). Even the smallest acts of kindness can really make a difference.

Decide to do one small act of kindness every single day for the next seven days. Here are some options: donate a few items of clothing to charity, pick up a few pieces of litter from your local area, put some spare change in a vending machine for the next user, write a thank you note to a loved one, text a friend you haven't spoken to in a while, or buy a few extra cans of food for your food bank.

It's cool to
be kind

Kindness is most definitely a good quality to cultivate.
Some people might find the concept of kindness a little
awkward or not in alignment with their tough persona, but
it's important that we all realize the power of kindness.

How would you feel if others described you as kind?
Explore any resistance you might have if you were
identified as a kind or helpful person.

There is always an opportunity to help others

There are so many wonderful ways in which you can help others. Many of them don't even require you to leave the comfort of your own home. There are lots of opportunities, both online and in person, to make a big difference.

Spend some time researching projects, movements, or activities that you could engage in to help others. You'll be amazed at what's out there.

As I help increase the joy of others, I naturally increase my own joy

As I mentioned earlier, you aren't responsible for other people's joy, as everyone should focus on making happiness an inside job. You can, however, help people feel good about themselves, which, in turn, makes you feel better about yourself.

Think of a loved one who could do with cheering up at the moment. Take the time today to do something special and unexpected for them.

I see the value in collaboration and community

Competition is important in certain areas of life, but we don't always have to apply it in our personal lives. We can be in competition with the people closest to us without realizing it. Choosing to collaborate and work with others can often be much more effective.

Who or what are you in competition with, without even initially realizing? How could you work to become more collaborative with these people or things, rather than fueling rivalry?

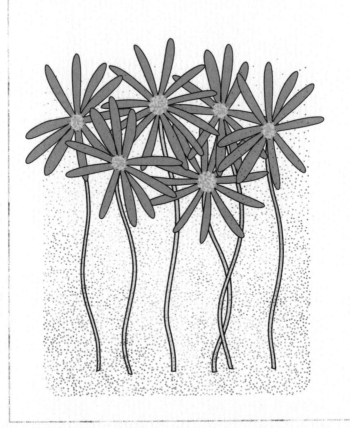

I make choices that are kinder to the planet

We all know that some aspects of our lives are not sustainable for the planet. It's important that we care for our environment too, so it's time to be honest about how we can change our actions to be kinder to the planet.

What daily changes can you make in order to be kinder to the environment? This could be recycling your plastics, creating a compost pile, or cleaning your street or local park.

I am a kind, generous, and considerate person

It's important that you see yourself as a good person. No matter what you have experienced, or what's happened in the past, you always have the option of changing the way you see yourself.

In what ways have you already demonstrated kindness, generosity, or consideration? Make a list in your journal. Or alternatively, how can you in the future show more generosity or consideration for others?

I have the ability to make a big impact

You are a powerful being. You have the ability to positively influence aspects of your own life as well as the lives of others. Don't underestimate the difference you can make.

A simple smile can have a huge impact. Try smiling at strangers as you go about your day today. Don't worry if you feel a little awkward at first. You might even want to add a greeting or a compliment. This has the potential to make someone's day.

The more I share, the more I gain

You don't need to hoard everything. Be open with your resources, time, or ideas. Rather than keeping things to yourself, see how it feels when you share whatever you feel comfortable sharing.

Try sharing something today. It might be a tip with your colleague, your food with someone who needs it more than you, or a few minutes with someone who needs a chat. Don't overextend yourself, but see how it makes you feel.

I am willing to become more selfless

To become more selfless means you are willing to consider others' needs before your own from time to time. This doesn't mean you completely abandon your own needs, but you might place them to the side for a moment to help someone who needs it.

Where do you think you are on a scale from selfish to selfless? What actions can you take to move closer to being selfless?

Good deeds will always find their way back to me

The more you put out into the world, the more you will receive. Some call it the law of cause and effect, or karma, which is essentially the idea that our actions matter. It might not always come back to you through the same person or event, but I do believe the more good you put out into the world, the more likely it is that you will receive some of that goodness back.

What blessings have you received in your life that could be the consequence of good deeds you carried out earlier in life?

I am always surrounded by love and support when I need it

When you take an interest and genuinely care about the well-being of others, it means that you're more likely to receive support when you need it. This is the benefit of being kind and helping others. It might not always come back to you through the same people, but I believe it always finds a way back.

Who has been there for you in times when you needed it most? How can you make sure you're there for others when they need support?

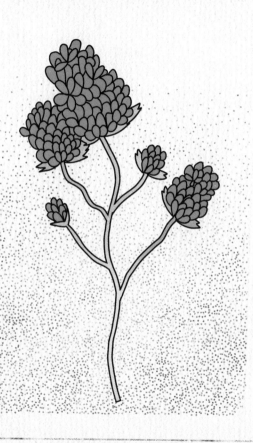

I inspire others to focus on their own happiness

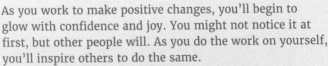

As you work to make positive changes, you'll begin to glow with confidence and joy. You might not notice it at first, but other people will. As you do the work on yourself, you'll inspire others to do the same.

Who else will benefit from all the positive changes you're making?

I choose to see the good that surrounds me

There are a lot of things wrong with this world, and of course there is a lot of suffering, but there's also a lot of goodness. You just have to open your eyes and be willing to look for it. The way I see it, we have to be optimistic. Every single human on this planet has hopes and dreams. This is what unites us. Hope is the fuel that keeps us going.

Are you willing to choose hope and optimism? If not, why?

My actions matter

It can be easy to think that even the small things we do for others won't really make a difference, but they truly do. Even if you don't see the immediate effects, don't be disheartened. Trust that you've made a positive impact.

Complete this sentence: My actions matter because . . .

I am excited to try new random acts of kindness

Helping others doesn't need to be so serious and time-consuming. Get creative and think of all the things you could do to put a smile on other people's faces.

Challenge yourself to try as many random acts of kindness as possible! Consider doing a thirty-day challenge with a friend who also wants to explore this.

I deserve to be here

The world needs exactly what you have to offer. You are truly unique, and your combination of traits and skills can really make a difference. You matter. You are important.

What traits, skills, or characteristics are you most proud of about yourself? How can you use your unique abilities to help those around you?

The only things that really matter are love and kindness

It's so easy to get caught up in stories of judgment, pain, fear, criticism, and doubt. It can seem like there are so many things that are wrong with us and the world around us. In the end, what really matters is how much you love and how kind you are.

What little things have you been overthinking that don't matter that much in the grand scheme of things?

I choose to spread joy instead of fear

It can be really easy to engage in conversations with others that promote gossip, fear, or uncertainty. Words are powerful, and these conversations can often leave everyone involved feeling worse than they did before.

How can you be more intentional with the words you say? Think about conversations with loved ones or friends, or even the content you share or create on social media. Are you promoting love and happiness, or inducing unpleasant feelings?

I choose to be kind to others, no matter where they are on their journey

Not everyone is working toward developing more kindness, happiness, and joy. Some people may respond to you with criticism, judgment, or any other manner of negativity. This really isn't personal. You have no idea what they have experienced, or what they might be currently going through.

Who in your life responds to you in negative ways? Have you been taking this personally? Try practicing compassion for these people, no matter how they respond to you.

Starting today, I'm committed to making the world a better place

You should be so proud of yourself for taking your happiness and well-being seriously and taking steps to increase your own joy and the joy of others. This is a lifelong journey, and every step can really make a difference to yourself and the collective.

How are you committed to making the world a better place? Consider sharing your thoughts and the actions you plan to take (no matter how big or small), whether that's with your family, friends, or followers. Happiness is contagious. Let's keep spreading it.

© 2022 by Quarto Publishing Group USA Inc.
Text and Illustrations © 2022 by Elicia Rose Trewick

First published in 2022 by Rock Point, an imprint of The Quarto Group,
142 West 36th Street, 4th Floor, New York, NY 10018, USA
T (212) 779-4972 F (212) 779-6058 www.Quarto.com

Rock Point titles are also available at discount for retail, wholesale, promotional, and bulk purchase. For details, contact the Special Sales Manager by email at specialsales@quarto.com or by mail at The Quarto Group, Attn: Special Sales Manager, 100 Cummings Center Suite 265D, Beverly, MA 01915 USA.

10 9 8 7 6 5 4 3 2 1

ISBN: 978-1-63106-868-3

Printed in China

Library of Congress Cataloging-in-Publication Data

Names: Trewick, Elicia Rose, author.
Title: Joy: 100 affirmations for happiness / Elicia Rose Trewick.
Other titles: Joy: a hundred affirmations for happiness
Description: New York, NY : Rock Point, 2022. | Series: Inspiring guides |
    Summary: "Feeling your best is made easy and simple with Joy: 100
    Affirmations for Happiness, your new ritual filled with positive
    affirmations and guided prompts to help you achieve personal growth"—
    Provided by publisher.
Identifiers: LCCN 2021061843 (print) | LCCN 2021061844 (ebook) | ISBN
    9781631068683 (hardcover) | ISBN 9780760376409 (ebook)
Subjects: LCSH: Joy. | Happiness. | Affirmations. | Self-actualization
    (Psychology)
Classification: LCC BF575.H27 T74 2022 (print) | LCC BF575.H27 (ebook) |
    DDC 158.1--dc23/eng/20220211
LC record available at https://lccn.loc.gov/2021061843
LC ebook record available at https://lccn.loc.gov/2021061844

Publisher: Rage Kindelsperger   Editor: Keyla Pizarro-Hernández
Creative Director: Laura Drew   Cover and Interior Design: Amy Sly
Managing Editor: Cara Donaldson

About the Author

Elicia Rose is a writer and illustrator based in Sheffield, England. She is the creator of Bloom Affirmations. What originally began as an Instagram page trying to make social media a kinder place to be has bloomed into an array of work focused on helping people feel better about themselves through the power of positive affirmations and journaling. Find out more at bloomaffirmations.com